Internet Marketing:

Grow Your Business, Build a Brand, Make Money Online and Sell Almost Anything!

William Swain

Copyright Notice

Disclaimer

Claim your FREE Audiobook Now

The Ultimate Guide to Make Money Onlines

Grab your chance to own this comprehensive two audiobook bundle by Max Lane, covering everything you need to know about how to make money online and passive income ideas.

Including:

- *Make Money Online: Twelve Proven Methods to Earn Passive Income and Work from Anywhere in the World*
- *The Fastlane to Make Money Online: How to Write a Book and Make Passive Income with Self Publishing, Audiobooks and More*

Do you want to learn how to make money online consistently? Without a lot of fuss, scams, or investing any money?

If so - you've come to the right place....

THE
ULTIMATE GUIDE
TO MAKE MONEY
ONLINE

Build a Passive Income Fortune with
Kindle Publishing, Amazon FBA, Affiliate
Marketing, Dropshipping, YouTube,
Udemy, Blogging, Shopify and much more

How You Can Go From Zero To $1,000/Month In The Next 30 Days...

Find Out More

In This Book You Will Discover

If you want more success, you need to start paying attention to and expand the things that give you the most leverage.

Introducing Internet Marketing

The Internet is a marketers dream come true as you have a low cost marketing tool that can reach a large audience. It will build your business fast.

No matter what business you're in, whether it's service related or manufactured goods you need to learn about internet marketing.

Internet Marketing defies all economic trends. In fact many internet marketers are generating 6 to 8 figure incomes working part time from the comfort of their homes. To be a successful internet marketer does not require a diploma or a degree. All you need is some free time, the right resources and training to start earning a passive income online.

Most people who start internet marketing fail due to the lack of quality resources. If you find yourself in that situation then don't worry; this book is going to teach you everything you need to know in order to develop any kind of internet marketing campaign with confidence.

Find Out:

- How to create profitable marketing campaigns
- Capture and close more Internet leads
- Know how to attract visitors and make them convert
- Drive consistent sales through email marketing
- Dominate social media with valuable content
- Drive on demand traffic to any website
- Engage with consumers more effectively online
- Build a brand that people love
- Charge high prices and have customers actually thank you for it
- And much, much more

Table of Contents

Introduction:
Now Is the Time to Cash In

If you are thinking about starting a business, you should consider setting up an internet marketing business. In this digital age wherein almost anything can be sold through the internet, the opportunities out there are endless. It's definitely easier to build a successful online business than a traditional business. A traditional business comes with a lot of responsibilities which are absent in an online business. For example, if you run an online business, you don't need to worry about rental expenses, utilities expenses, or heavy overhead costs. Everything is online, in the virtual space.

Another great reason why now is the time to start an internet marketing business is the fact that the web offers tons of tools and resources that you can utilize. Not only that but often for free. For instance, you have access to immensely popular networking sites like Facebook, Twitter, and Instagram. These are sites that are free to use and attract billions of users. Chances are your target customers are active in these sites. You can reach these potential customers by merely being active on social media. Free social sites are just the tip of the iceberg. There are other tools, resources, and platforms online that you can use as leverage in building and growing your internet marketing business.

Here's what you should always keep in mind. The internet is a low-cost tool that you can use to market and sell almost anything. It doesn't matter if you are selling a service or a manufactured product. The methods of promoting your goods are pretty much the same. And you have access to a global marketplace.

You can choose to sell your goods to anyone. That customer can be a student in Melbourne, Australia or a farmer in Scotland. It's even easier if you are selling a digital product. One that you can deliver to a customer remotely through the internet (i.e. downloadable ebooks and software).

Anyone can start an internet marketing business. There are no qualifications or prior experience required. Don't have a college degree? No problem. A huge number of successful online entrepreneurs didn't even finish high school. Don't have any experience in computer programming? No problem. You don't need to be a technical genius to create a successful business website. The point here is that there are very little barriers to building a successful online business. If you work smart, you can achieve all your business goals. The information is all here for you to discover.

You can even choose to run your internet marketing business as a part-time operation. That means you don't have to leave your main job. You can always work on your online business in your free time. That's the beauty of online entrepreneurship. You own your time. You can work on your business only when you have to. No one is forcing you to wake up at 6:00 am and work until 5:00 pm. You are your own boss, basically.

Building a successful online business is 100% achievable. However, for that to happen, you need to start properly. Starting properly means you must have the resources and the knowledge to make sure that you are heading in the right direction. That's the reason why I've written this book you are currently reading. I'm here to help you get started in the right direction.

In this book, you are going to learn about the basics of internet marketing. I'm going to provide you with all the necessary information you need to start, build, grow, and scale a successful internet marketing business. After reading this book, you should be more than equipped to start a business and grow it to the levels you want. Think of this book as your ultimate guide in your entrepreneurial journey. Let's get going.

Chapter 1:
How to Recognize Your Target Market

This is where the journey begins. You can't start an online business without identifying who your customers will be. You may have the best product or service idea but this amounts to nothing if there's no viable market for it.

With that said, don't build a business around a product or service if you haven't done your market research. Doing market research isn't that difficult. Again, there are many tools and resources online that you can use as leverage for your market research. Most of these tools and resources are also free to use. Make use of tools such as Google trends to identify what is hot online now. Then make use of Google keywords to zoom in on profitable keywords and terms.

Market research can be a complicated process depending on the nature of the business you have in mind. However, allow me to simplify the process. There are six major steps in the market research process. These are as follows:

1. Define your target customer and his/her persona.
2. Understand the characteristics, challenges, and buying habits of your target customer.
3. Engage your target customers to learn from them.
4. Come up with research questions that you can ask your target customers.
5. List and understand your potential competitors.
6. Summarize your research findings.
7. Answer the following question based on your research findings:
Is there a profitable market for your product or service idea?

Let's discuss these steps in more detail.

1. Define your target customer and his/her persona.

You must first understand who your target customers are. As I have mentioned earlier, don't just pursue a business idea because you think that there will be buyers for your product or service. So many would be entrepreneurs have this great idea but without testing it your risking losing time and money.

First off you have to test the idea if it's viable. But how exactly are you going to do that? This is the beginning of your market research. The first thing you should do is write down a quick list of who you think your customers will be. For example, let's say that you have written a tutorial ebook about woodworking. Just off the top of your head, who are the people you think would be interested in purchasing your ebook?

You can list down carpenters, furniture creators, interior decorators, artists, woodworking students, arts and crafts students, and stay-at-home dads as your target market. This is pretty obvious because these are the people who are most likely in need of a guide book about woodworking. They represent those who will likely find value in what you have written in the book. Go over the list a few times to make sure that you have written down all those who would be interested in your product or service.

2. Understand the characteristics, challenges, and buying habits of your target customer.

Now that you have an idea of who your target customers are, the next step is to perform what is referred to as secondary research. In this step, you are going to attempt to verify if your instincts are right. Were you correct in assuming that the people in the list you made will be interested in buying your product or service? In this step, you are no longer going to rely on your instincts. You need to take your market research further by using tools and resources to gather data about your target market.

Remember that your goal here is to identify the characteristics, challenges, and buying habits of your potential customers. This means that you need to collect data about all of these factors. One of the most important tools you can use is a keyword research tool. There are dozens of these tools online. Some are free to use and some are subscription-based. If you are just starting out, I highly recommend that you make use of Google's own keyword research tool. It's 100% free to use. It's very comprehensive. And it offers the most accurate data. That is of course expected given the fact that Google commands more than 60% of online searches.

A keyword research tool helps you understand your potential customers. Where are they coming from? What words and phrases are they using to look for your products and services? What demographics do they belong to? These are just some of the important questions that you can find answers to using a keyword research tool.

3. Engage your target customers to learn from them.

If you have performed step 1 and 2, then you have a clear idea of who your customers are and where they are coming from. What you are going to do next is to engage your potential customers to further learn about them and their needs. Identify the places online where they congregate and hang out. You then get inside these platforms and be among them. Such platforms include social media sites (i.e. Facebook, Twitter, YouTube, and Instagram), blogs, and forums.

Let's take Facebook for example. The social networking site has the Groups feature where people who share the same interests can join and interact in a group page. What you do is find group pages that are very relevant to your product or service, join the pages, and engage with the members. You can learn a lot by simply browsing through the posts and comments in the pages. What topics are they talking about? What products and services are often mentioned in the discussions? As you go through the discussions, make notes of the important details about your target customers.

4. Come up with research questions that you can ask your target customers.

This step involves writing down questions or creating surveys and convincing your potential customers to answer them. There are two ways on how you can do surveys. You can do the surveys yourself or you can outsource the process to a survey company. There are so many of these survey companies around today. However, some survey companies are notorious for using unviable respondents which will obviously lead to misleading data. With that said, I recommend that you perform the surveys yourself. For decent results, you don't have to gather a ton of respondents.

5. List and understand your potential competitors.

You also need to understand your competition. This is something that a lot of new online entrepreneurs often take for granted. Having a high-quality product or service does not guarantee online success. You may have a great product but what if there are hundreds of other great products out there that are very similar to yours? Or if you are competing with huge brands and personalities. The general rule in starting an online business is that you should only enter a particular niche or industry if you are confident that you can compete in the arena.

This is why it's very important that you do competitor research. How tough is the competition in the niche you are targeting? Are you up against established brands or corporations? Are you up against small business operations? Can you offer a product or service that is much better or more affordable compared to the competition? These are some of the questions you should ask yourself when reviewing your competition. Your main goal in researching about your competition is to determine if you can compete against them should you decide to pursue your business idea.

6. Summarize your research findings.

If you have accomplished all of the previous steps, you should have in front of you a mountain of data that pertain to your target market and potential competitors. The next obvious step is to go through all your findings and data and summarize the information so that you can take the proper actions. If you have done your research properly, it shouldn't be that hard to draw clear and actionable conclusions from the information you have gathered.

It's best to put your summary into writing so that you can go over it and review it whenever it's necessary. Keep in mind that the summary of your research findings form the foundation upon which you are going to decide whether it's viable to pursue your business idea or not. Make sure that your summary stays true to the findings of your research.

7. Answer the following question based on your research findings: Is there a profitable market for your product or service idea?

This is it. This is where you finally decide if there's a market for your proposed product or service. After doing the market research, collecting data, organizing your findings, and writing down a summary of your findings, you now have to decide if the idea can be turned into a profitable business. Is there a market for the product or service? The answer should be a "yes" before you can move forward. If it's a "no", then you need to start from the bottom.

The whole point of this chapter is that it's very important to conduct market research before you decide to pursue a business idea. You have to be sure that there are people who will be interested in buying your product or service. The only way for you to know this is to conduct a thorough market research.

Chapter 2: Understanding the Brand That You Want To Build

There was a time when the words "brand" and "branding" were associated with major companies and multi-million dollar corporations. When people spoke of brands, they spoke about the likes of Nike or Colgate or Nestle or Ford Motors. Those days are over. Thanks to technology and the coming of the digital age, you don't have to be a multi-million company to be considered a brand. Small and medium-sized businesses now have the chance to build their own brands and compete with major corporations. This is one of the biggest reasons why there's a growing number of online entrepreneurs. Today, even a single person can be considered a brand. If you have a sizable following online, you are considered a brand. That's how powerful online marketing can be.

Anyway, since we are talking about internet marketing businesses here, let's talk about how you can transform your business idea into a successful brand. Again, we need to remind you that branding these days no longer requires a lot of money. Branding is no longer about purchasing expensive ads in television or erecting giant billboards or hiring celebrity brand ambassadors. You have to get rid of this notion that you are going to need a ton of cash in order to successfully build a brand.

Online branding is a completely different ball game. What you need is a good product or service and a practical branding strategy. Basically, online branding is about using tools and resources available in the internet with the aim of positioning your brand in a specific marketplace. For example, let's say that you are selling an app that creates digital calendars and schedules for people who want to organize their time. Branding your app entails creating enough hype and online chatter so that when people talk about apps for calendars and schedules, they will be talking about you. They will be talking about your brand in the same sense that consumers talk about Colgate when they discuss about toothpaste products.

In a nutshell, branding is a very powerful technique and you should be spending a good amount of your time and resources on it if you want your online business to be successful. Building your online brand isn't going to be easy. That's something you should expect especially if you are entering a competitive niche where there's a lot of already established brands. Growing your brand is also going to take some time so you need to be patient. You can't build a successful brand overnight.

Before you begin with your online branding campaign, you must have a clear understanding of what type of brand you want to pursue. You have to define the persona or culture that you want to present to customers. For example, The North Face brands itself as an outdoors company that is adventurous and is a risk-taker. Patagonia, on the other hand, brands itself as an outdoors company that is socially-responsible by donating a portion of its profits to environmental causes. LinkedIn brands itself as the social networking site for professionals and entrepreneurs.

The bottomline here is that you must have a branding goal. How do you want your customers to perceive you? It's a lot easier to implement a branding campaign if you and your team clearly understand your branding goals.

Here are some of the most effective ways on how you can grow your online brand:

1. Create a branding theme for all your online operations and activities.
Everything you do that is related to your online business should have some form of cohesiveness. Creating a branding theme is a rather broad term but it basically means doing all things with your branding goals in mind. For example, if you want your consumers to perceive you as a fun and carefree business, then all of your marketing and promotional efforts should be fun, light-hearted, and humorous. Furthermore, you should not forget details like the colors you use in your marketing materials. A good example is Coke and the color red. Have you ever wondered why Coke uses the color red in all of its marketing materials? It's because the color red is a major aspect of the company's branding theme.

2. Design and create a professional logo for your online business and use it in all your online communications and sales operations. Needless to say, your logo is a critical component of your brand's identification. Your logo is the symbol that represents who you are as a business or as a company. When customers see your logo, they are quickly reminded of your products, services, and what you stand for as a business.

With that said, it's important that you invest in a unique and high-quality business logo. Remember that your logo will be used in all materials that you use online. The logo should be a proper representation of your business and your products and services. If you don't have any background in logo design or graphics design, it's best that you outsource the creation of your logo. There are literally thousands of experienced and highly-skilled graphic designers out there who can create your logo for you.

3. Make use of a branded email signature.
You are an online business so majority of your communications with customers, business partners, and other concerned parties will be through email. You will probably be sending dozens if not hundreds of emails every single day depending on the size of your business. In short, your email signature is a powerful branding tool. You can add in your signature the name of your business, your logo, contact details, an RSS feed, or even links to your various social media pages. There are apps and tools like Wisestamp that can make the job easier for you. Using the tools allow you to create and customize great email signatures.

4. Use social media as a leverage.
Social media sites are probably the most powerful online branding tools today. According to recent statistics from the Pew Research Center, more than 75% of adults use social networking sites. That's huge. It means that if you want to reach as many people as possible with your branding message, you need to be on social media. You need to be on the biggest players in the social media scene like

Facebook, Twitter, Instagram, LinkedIn, Pinterest, and YouTube. All of these social sites are free to use so there's no reason why you shouldn't sign up with them. You have very little to lose in using them to advance your branding goals.

5. Come up with an interesting and catchy slogan or tagline.

Just like your business logo, your slogan will be used in nearly all of your communication and marketing materials. Your slogan should be unique, short, straight to the point, and memorable. Furthermore, it should reflect the identity and brand of your business. Here's a quick rundown of some of the most well-known slogans and the businesses behind such slogans. Use these slogans as an inspiration in coming up with your own.

I'm lovin' it. – McDonalds
Just do it. – Nike
Have a break, have a Kit Kat – Kit Kat
Taste the rainbow. – Skittles
Eat fresh. – Subway
Don't be evil. – Google
Think different. – Apple
Impossible is nothing. – Adidas
The king of beers. – Budweiser

6. Add credibility to your brand by publishing testimonials in your websites and social media pages.

Testimonials are formal statements from customers, business partners, and other concerned parties that testify about the quality of your products and services.

A testimonial can come from anywhere. It could be from a review written by a blogger. It could be from a review posted on a social site like Facebook. It could be from a letter sent to you via email. Testimonials are very powerful boosters for your business especially if you get a few from well-known names in your niche. For example, if you are selling a bicycle spare part and you get a testimonial from Lance Armstrong, your sales will surely hit the roof.

7. Start a blog.

This is one of the smartest things you can do for your business. Starting a blog is very easy. You can set up one in just a few minutes. You can host the blog inside your main website or you can get a separate domain for it. You also have the choice of using free blogging platforms like Wordpress, Tumblr, and Blogspot. As you can see, there are very little barriers to creating a blog. However, building a readership for your blog can be difficult. But if you consistently publish great content, your blog should grow a lot faster. The general role in blogging is that you should focus on topics that relate to your products and services. It's absolutely okay to go out of topic every once in a while but you shouldn't overdo it because going out of topic is one of the biggest reasons why readers lose interest in a blog.

8. Give your brand a face.

What does this mean? It literally means what it says. You should show your face as the owner and manager of the business. If you run the business with several people, you can also consider showing their faces. The best way to do this is to put photos of yourselves in the bio sections or about pages in your websites. Consumers tend to trust businesses that aren't afraid to show the faces of their owners. Invest in professional photos. If your not comfortable being the face of the brand, hire talent.

9. Develop a customer reward plan.
Building a brand isn't just about attracting new customers, it's also about making sure that your current customers continue supporting your business down the line. One of the best ways to nurture customer loyalty is by giving them rewards. There are so many ways on how you can reward customers for their loyalty and patronage. You can offer discounts for customers who reach a certain purchase threshold. You can offer freebies. You can come up with membership programs wherein members have access to promos and discounts that non-members don't have access to.

10. Advertise your business.
Advertising is deeply enmeshed with branding. You have to be engaged in it if you really want to get the word out about your business. Advertising is a necessity especially if you are just starting out which means only a few people know about your products and services. Creating targeted ads will attract your initial waves of customers. The great thing about online advertising is that it's really affordable. It's not as expensive as advertising in traditional media outlets like newspapers, magazines, and television programs. With a small and limited budget, you still have the potential to reach thousands if not millions of target customers.

These strategies aren't that difficult to implement. They take time to generate results, that's for sure. But as we have mentioned earlier, branding doesn't happen overnight. Patience is the key to success here. Think of Coca-Cola and their branding strategies. They've been doing it from the first day the company was set up. Several decades later, they are still following these branding strategies. That's patience. That's consistency. The same principles can be applied to branding an internet marketing business no matter how small or big it is.

Chapter 3:
How to Write a Comprehensive and Realistic Internet Business Plan

Don't start an internet business if you don't have a business plan. Ask any expert for advice and this is what they would tell you. Building a business without a plan is a recipe for failure. Don't get too overconfident about your business idea and products. If you want to start right, you should sit down first and write down your business plan. We are talking about small to medium-sized businesses here so all you need are the basic sections of a business plan. You can even write a concrete business plan in a few hours depending on the size of your business idea and the range of products you intend on selling.

Here's a quick overview of the most basic elements of a business plan:

1. Executive Summary
This is a concise overview of your business plan. It must be well-written, clear, and straight to the point. A person reading the executive summary should be able to get a clear understanding of what your business is about and what you intend to accomplish with it. The executive summary should contain your business name and location, a quick description of your products and services, your mission and vision statements, and the specific purpose of the plan. Most entrepreneurs would suggest that you write the executive summary last so that you can include important information from the other sections of the business plan.

2. Business or Company Description
If you are proposing the business idea to a potential partner or someone who can help you with funding,

this is usually the section that read first because it's where their interests lie. With that said, you should make sure that this section is written properly and completely. The contents of this section may include the following:
- A quick summary of your short-term and long-term business goals
- The legal structure of your business
- A summary of your company's projected growth including your market and financial highlights
- A summary of your products, services, suppliers, and target customers
- A brief description of your business model, the nature of your operations, and the needs and demands of your business with regard supply.

3. Product and Service Description
Clearly describe the products you are selling or the services that you are offering. This doesn't have to be very detailed. Just make sure that a person reading the section can clearly determine what you are offering and the value you are providing. You should also include in this section some information about suppliers, manufacturers, costs, and estimated revenue you can generate from your sales. If possible, you should consider including high-quality photos of the line of products you are selling. This is very important if you are going to present the business plan to a potential business partner or fund provider.

4. Market Analysis
This is where you provide realistic data about your target market, your competition, and the state of the market you want to penetrate. The contents of this

section should come from a thorough market research that you have completed previously. You don't have to put all your findings here. Just create a summary of your findings. You can put the raw data in the appendix section. Your market analysis should include an evaluation of the strengths and weaknesses of your competition, a sketch of your targeted customer segments, a description of the current outlook in your niche, and projected marketing data for your services and products.

5. Organization and Management Team

This is where you create an outline of your company's organizational structure. That basically means identifying the owners, the partners, the management team, and the board of directors if there's any. You should come up with a simple organizational chart with descriptions of your key employees and business departments. Put yourself in the shoes of a potential employee or management team member. If you are looking at the organizational chart, you should be able to easily identify where you are in it and what your roles and responsibilities are.

6. Sales and Marketing Strategies

This is one of the most important sections of your business plan because the success of your proposed business will greatly depend on what you've written in this section. You need to offer a comprehensive description of your marketing and sales strategy. How do you intend to drive and increase sales? What are the online platforms you are going to use in your marketing campaigns? Which of these platforms will receive priority from you? Who are the people who will be responsible for implementing your sales and marketing strategies. These are some of the questions you have to answer in this section of the business plan.

7. Funding Requirements

In this section, you provide information how you are going to fund your business operations. Where are you getting the money? What's your funding model? Who are your potential credit providers? How are you going to repay these funds? These are the questions you are going to answer in this section of the business plan. You should include information for a worst-case scenario or a best-case scenario. There should be a plan A and a plan B for your funding requirements. If your funding dries up, there should be options for you on where you are going to seek more funding.

8. Financial Projections

This section of the business plan can be very complicated and technical. With that said, you are going to need the services of an accountant. You should only come up with your financial projections after you have completed your market research and analysis. Additionally, you should have already set goals for your business. Your financial projections will depend on these things. An accountant can't make financial projections of he doesn't understand your goals or the current state of your target market.

9. Appendix

Although this is an important part of the business plan, you have the option to include it or remove it from the main body of the business plan. Why?

Because the appendix contains some confidential and proprietary information that shouldn't be viewed by anyone. With that said, you can decide to provide the appendix for a reader on an as-needed basis. For example, if a potential business partner wants to see detailed data about how you conducted your market research, then you can provide that person a copy of the appendix. Creditors or anyone who is helping you with the funding might ask for information that's contained in the appendix. Be ready to provide the information to them.

What you've read above is but a simplified version of an internet marketing business plan. These are just the basic sections of a business plan. You are free to add more sections as you deem necessary. You can also choose to break down each section into what's considered as sub-sections. The choice is yours. Be sure to spend some time here as it will give you the blueprint for your business. However don't get lost in the details.

Chapter 4:
How to Create Workable and Profitable Internet Marketing Campaigns

After setting up and launching your internet marketing business, the next obvious step is to start with your online campaigns with the ultimate goals of attracting visitors and converting them into paying customers. Of course, this is easier said than done. In the following guide, we are going to provide you with simple strategies and tips on how to create, run, and manage your internet marketing campaigns. Running an online campaign is going to cost you some money and if you don't get the results you wanted, then that basically means you are operating at a loss. With that said, you need to be serious about your online marketing campaigns.

When it comes to online campaigns, planning is everything. I'm assuming that you've completed your market research which means you only have to come up with marketing strategies on how to reach your identified target market. This is where you create a plan on how you are going to execute these strategies. Planning and proper execution. These are the main ingredients of a successful internet marketing campaign.

Choosing Your Marketing Channels
There are dozens of methods on how you can deliver your marketing message in front of your potential customers. Let's refer to these methods as marketing channels. What you need to do is go over these channels and find the ones that you think are a good fit for your business and your business model. Which of these channels do you think have the ability to turn your audience from prospects into paying customers?

It can be tempting to try and use all of the channels you have access to. But trying everything at once will actually hurt your business instead of helping it. I would recommend that you choose three to five marketing channels and focus your efforts on them first. Using just a few selected channels makes sense because you can devote your time and resources on them. For example, you can choose to focus on search engine optimization, social media marketing, and advertising as your main marketing channels. Each of these channels has its own inherent complexities. In fact, using all three platforms will already have your hands full.

My point here is that you need to choose a few marketing channels and dedicate your time, focus, and resources on them. Don't ever make the mistake of assuming that the more platforms you use, the more effective your marketing campaign will be. This isn't the case at all. In fact, online entrepreneurs who devote their attention on a few platforms and channels tend to accomplish more than those who use too many channels.

Deciding on Your Marketing Budget
A common mistake among new online entrepreneurs is that they start marketing their products and services without taking into account first their marketing budget. In most cases, they end up spending more than they can afford. To ensure that you don't go beyond your means, you should set up a realistic budget for your marketing campaigns. You should stick to that budget no matter what happens.

There's no standard procedure on calculating your marketing budget because it depends on a lot of factors like the size of your business, the type of products and services you are selling, the marketing channels you have chosen, and the niche you are trying to penetrate. For example, if you plan on advertising your products but you have a limited budget, you might consider advertising on social media sites instead of advertising through Google Ads. This is because advertising on social sites is usually a lot cheaper compared to the Google Ads program.

Try to give your budgets a specific time period. For example, you can set aside $200 a week for advertising on Facebook, $50 a day for advertising on Google Ads, or $1000 a month for direct advertising in blogs and websites that are relevant to your business. You need to be working with real numbers and specific budget estimates. It's okay if you get the amounts wrong during your initial marketing campaigns. It happens to most online marketers. You will get better in setting up budgets as you learn more about the industry and as you gain more experience.

Execution through the Marketing Channels You Have Chosen

After choosing your marketing channels and coming up with your budget, what's left to do is to execute your marketing plan. This is where a lot of new online entrepreneurs stumble and fail. They may have a good plan and a well thought-out budget but they can't seem to pull the trigger to generate results. You see, executing a marketing plan isn't just about following the plan. It's also about adjusting your tactics if things aren't going as you expected. For example, you have chosen Facebook as a marketing channel. However, you soon realized that you aren't generating traffic or leads from the networking site as per your marketing projections.

So what should you do next? You pause your Facebook marketing efforts and spend some time to determine what is wrong. Why aren't you getting the results you want? Why are Facebook users not engaging with your marketing messages and ads? Find these problems and attempt to fix them. You also can't discount the possibility that maybe Facebook isn't just the right platform for the type of online business you have.

When promoting your business through different marketing channels, you should make it a point to follow the specific rules, policies, and guidelines that each channel requires from you. You are using platforms by third parties. If you do something that is against any of their rules and policies, you can get banned from the platform.

You should also take the time to track and measure the results you generate from each marketing channel. Tracking helps you determine which marketing channels are generating the most results for your business. For example, after tracking your marketing campaigns, you find out that social media marketing platforms capture internet leads more efficiently than other channels. This is a cue for you to ramp up your efforts in the social media sector of your campaigns.

Keep a record of all your results and measure them against the goals for each campaign. Include all of your spendings and actions. This will help you really zone in on what works and cut what doesn't.

Again, you need to be patient with your internet marketing campaigns. Take it slow and don't make decisions if you are not that sure about the results or if there are too many risks involved.

Chapter 5:
How to Use SEO to Fast-Track the Growth of Your Internet Business

Search engine optimization or SEO is something you should be knowledgeable about if you want to be a successful online entrepreneur. Always keep in mind the fact that majority of consumers who shop online usually start their search on Google. If you don't rank well on Google, there's a slim chance that your target customers will ever find out about your products and services. The only way for you to get to the top of the search results is through effective SEO.

In this chapter, we are going to discuss the most effective strategies that you can use to improve your rankings in Google and other search engines. Implementing SEO isn't as complicated nor technical as you might think. It can be frustrating at first but it gets much easier as you learn more about the process. Anyway, below are some tips on how you can optimize your website and make it rank better in the search results.

1. Make sure that your website is user-friendly.

This is the first thing that you should do. Review your website and make sure that it's running smoothly and loading quickly. Nothing turns off visitors faster than a website that takes forever to load. See to it that all your links are working properly. Broken links are a big no-no for search engines. Another aspect of your website that you should fine-tune is the navigation. A visitor should be able to get from one page to another with ease. You should have simple and clear navigation tabs either at the top or on the side bar of your website.

2. Don't forget to perform comprehensive research about the keywords and phrases that you are going to use.

A lot of new online entrepreneurs often make the mistake of skipping this part. Keyword research and development is the foundation of your SEO strategy. You can't move forward with your optimization campaign if you don't have a list of keywords and phrases that you are going to target. All aspects of your optimization campaign will depend on these keywords. Whether you are doing content marketing or link building, you have to make use of your targeted keywords. If it's your first time to perform keyword research, we highly recommend that you use Google's own keyword planner. It's free to use. You can just sign in with your Gmail account.

3. Create sitemaps for your website.

This will help in making sure that search engines index the contents of your website. It's best that you create both XML and HTML versions of the sitemap. A sitemap allows the crawlers sent in by the search engines to reach all areas and sections of your website. A sitemap is especially necessary if you have a lot of archived content. There are sitemap generators that you can use to easily create sitemaps for your websites.

4. Make your site mobile-friendly.

You have to be aware of the fact that a huge number of people these days use their mobile phones to search about products and services online. If your website is not mobile-friendly, then you are missing out on a huge market. Having a mobile-friendly website is also a plus point for search engines like Google. The first step to make your website mobile-friendly is to make sure that it has a responsive design. If a person accesses the website through his phone, the design adjusts and adapts depending on the screen size of the mobile device.

5. Keep building authoritative backlinks for your website.

Your website will rank higher in the search results if readers perceive it as trustworthy and authoritative. And one of the best ways to build online authority and trust is through proper link building. If other websites are linking back to your website, this means that they are giving you votes on trustworthiness and credibility. Google and other search engines look at these links and consider them when deciding how your website should rank in the search results. However, you should focus your backlinking efforts on attracting links from credible websites. Quality matters more than quantity. Getting one link from a credible website is better than getting ten links from ten spammy sites.

6. Install a SSL certificate on your website.

Online security is valued by Google especially these days wherein hackers are getting more blatant with their attacks. The point here is that Google will take into account the overall security of your website when determining how you should rank in the search results. Suffice it to say that if you have a secure website, you have better chances at ranking higher. With an SSL certificate, your website will be more secure for users and this boosts your site's credibility. Installing an SSL certificate is highly recommended especially if your site collects sensitive data (i.e. personal details, credit card numbers, passwords) from users.

7. Make use of SEO-friendly URLs.

Crawlers sent in by the search engines also look for clues in your URLs. The general rule is that it's better if you have descriptive URLs. They should be readable and they should contain keywords and phrases that are relevant to the contents of the page. For example, if the page is about social media marketing, it should contain the words social media and marketing.

8. Don't use Flash.

There's a reason why SEO experts always advise website owners to not use Flash in their websites. Of course, you can use Flash if it's absolutely necessary but you should tone down your usage of it. Flash is bad for SEO, it's that simple. Not only will Flash significantly slow down the loading speed of the website, crawlers also find it very difficult to index content and pages that contain Flash. Last but not the least; don't use Flash because it has a long history of security flaws, bugs, and malware. As we have discussed earlier, less secure websites are red flags for search engines.

9. Maintain a constant flow of high-quality content.

When it comes to content marketing, consistency is key. This is especially true if you are running a blog or a website that's similar to a blog. The more valuable content you churn out, the more visitors you attract. Mix up the type of content you produce. Don't just focus on creating articles, you should also create photos, videos, and infographics to make your website more appealing to various readers.

10. Connect your website with your social media pages.

Search engines now take into account social media chatter when ranking websites. If a website gets a lot of mentions and discussions in social sites like Facebook or Twitter, it is considered as more credible. These social media signs provide the website with more reasons to rank better in the search results.

If implemented properly and regularly, these practical SEO strategies can get your website closer to your ranking goals. If you attract more visitors from organic searches, you can close more sales. The growth of your business will be faster if you are getting a large chunk of your web traffic from search engines like Google and Bing.

Chapter 6:
Practical Tips for Generating Massive Traffic Towards Your Business Website

Traffic generation is not rocket science. It may take some time to master all the tricks but you will get there. Driving traffic to your website is something that you should take seriously. You should spend several hours every day on traffic generation especially if your internet business has just launched. You can make more money online if you master the art of attracting high-quality traffic. To help you get started, here's a rundown of the most effective methods you should be using.

1. Optimize your website for the search engines (i.e. Google, Bing).

I've discussed SEO in Chapter 5 so you should definitely go over that chapter again. SEO is very powerful in letting people know that your business and your products exist. Truth be told, SEO is the foundation of search marketing. Not only is it a way of attracting traffic, it's also a way to make sure that you remain competitive. If your competitors are better in optimizing their websites, then you will be losing out your customers to them.

2. Try email marketing.

Almost everyone who uses the internet has an email address. This is because you can't use a lot of online services if you don't have an email address. In order to market effectively via email, you should set up a newsletter so that you can start building your email list. People who subscribe to your newsletter are automatically added to your list. Through the newsletter, you update your subscribers about the latest developments in your business (i.e. new product announcements). Attract subscribers through lead marketing. Essentially, you can set up websites with free offers in exchange for an email address.

3. Set up a blog for your business website.
You can either build a blog inside your main website or you can set up a separate domain for it. A blog is a great platform for creating extra content for both loyal customers and potential customers. It also happens that blogs are loved by search engines which means they rank really well in the search results. If you are consistently updating it then your going to rank really well for your search terms.

4. Engage with your customers online.
Don't forget to interact with your customers. If they send you emails, make it a point to answer them. If they leave comments in your website or in your blog, respond whenever you can. The goal here is to let your customers know that you genuinely care about their concerns. Don't just be all about posting and never interacting. Effective internet marketing is a two way conversation between you and your customers.

5. Use the Analytics tool to understand how visitors are interacting with your website.
There's a lot of reasons why you should use the Google Analytics tool. First of all, it's free so you have nothing to lose in taking advantage of it. But the most important reason why you should use it is that it provides you with valuable insights about your website visitors. You can learn about where your visitors are coming from, which links they are clicking, which sections of your website are getting the most

attention, and which external websites are referring traffic to your website.

6. Write content for other websites as a guest writer.

This is called content marketing. You produce content with the goal of having these published in other websites. In return for the free content, the host website puts a link within the content or within the author bio that links back to your own website. Collaboration is an excellent way of building more interest in your brand whilst also making connections with experienced people who can even mentor and lift you up. Reach out to influencers in your field.

7. Create a landing page.

This is a great strategy if you are selling products. You create landing pages for the products. You optimize these landing pages to attract visitors from search engines and other sources like social media sites. When a visitor gets to the landing page, you have them redirected to your main website. For this reason, most online marketers utilize several landing pages depending on the number of products or services they are selling.

8. Be active in social media.

Chances are most of your target customers are using social networks like Facebook, Twitter, Instagram, YouTube, etc. You should take the time to engage with your customers through these sites. Social media enables you to connect with your target audience in a more open and personal manner. This build trust and loyalty over time.

9. Advertise your business and products on social media.

Engaging with people on social media is great but if you want to double or triple your social media reach, you should consider buying ads in the platforms you are using. The good news is that the biggest social media platforms today like Facebook, Twitter, and Instagram have their own advertising programs. Through these advertising programs, you can boost the reach of our posts, updates, and tweets. Advertising on social media these days can be incredibly rewarding since you are able to zone in on specifics such as location, age and interest. Utilize your market research to build effective advertising campaigns.

10. Advertise online using Google Ads.

Google has the best advertising program online. So if you want to advertise your website, you should definitely use their program. It's very affordable as well and you have complete control over your budget. You don't have to pay more than you can afford. You can make use of Google Keywords tool to identify the best keywords to implement.

11. Submit your content to aggregator sites.

A content aggregator is a type of social networking site that collects and curates content from all over the web. Content in these sites are user-generated which means anyone can register and submit content. Great examples of aggregator websites include Reddit, Feedly, Panda, Techmeme, Metacritic, and PopUrls.

12. Give out freebies.

Everybody loves free items. It doesn't matter if it's a free ebook, a free shirt, or a free gift voucher. People will be lining up to get their hands on them. Use the free item as a front to entice people to visit your website. You can promote the giveaway outside of your website but for people to be eligible to receive it, they need to visit your website first.

13. Run online contests.

This is one of the most powerful ways on how to build hype for your business. A successful contest can attract thousands of new visitors to your website. To promote your online contests, you should use as leverage several marketing channels like social media and paid advertising.

14. Create free online courses then use these as leverage to attract more people.

You can offer your knowledge and expertise for free in the guise of online courses. People who like your courses will likely search for more content from you by visiting your website. It's all about building trust and adding value. If they like what you do and become a fan of yours than that is likely to lead to revenue for your business.

I am not in any way suggesting that you should use every single one of these methods. How many of these methods you are going to implement will depend on the amount of time you have in your hands. What I would suggest is that you find the methods that generate the best results for your website. Experiment and then ramp up your efforts on these specific methods to scale the results.

Chapter 7:
How to Convert Website Visitors into Paying Customers

Enticing people to visit your website is just the first step in online sales. Driving traffic is important but you should also learn how to convert your visitors into paying customers. This is a lot more difficult to do because you don't have control over the spending capabilities of your visitors. However, there are things you can do to increase the chances that a visitor buys something from you.

Keep the Navigation Simple
Don't you find it frustrating when you visit a shopping website and you can't seem to get around as quickly as you would like? The site navigation is so undefined that you waste a lot of time trying to find which tabs you should click. This is a serious problem that can scare away a lot of potential buyers. You should review your website and make sure that the navigation system is as smooth and clear as possible.

Highlight Your Products and Services
This is obviously a no-brainer but a lot of new online entrepreneurs tend to take it for granted. You should use a website design that prominently displays your offers. Think of your website as the front facade of a physical store. Your best products should be prominently displayed front and center. Implementing this simple rule can quickly increase your conversion rate especially if you receive a lot of your traffic from search engines.

Make Use of Customer Testimonials
You can improve your conversion rate by simply featuring customer testimonials in your website. As much as possible, you should only use independent

and verifiable testimonials. For example, if a blogger posted a good review of product or service in his blog, you can use quotes from the review as testimonials for your products. You can also use reviews and comments left by your customers in your social media pages. The main point in publishing testimonials is to provide your potential clients of the potential value that they can get from your product/service.

Offer Lots of Freebies

When you offer a freebie, most consumers would look at it as a bonus. Research studies show that when a product is tied up with a bonus, the likelihood that the customer purchases the product can increase by up to two-fold. To make the freebie even more difficult to turn down, you can provide a limited time period for the freebie. For example, the freebie can only be available to customers who buy it from January 1 to January 30. The limited timeframe makes the customer feel like he might miss out should he decide not to buy the item right now.

Make Sure That the Visitor Understands the Value of Your Offers

For every product or service that you list in your website, you should provide a detailed description of it. The aim is to inform the customer about the product's value and how it can help him. This is where your sales pitch skills come into play. Don't just say "buy this" or "buy that", you should provide reasons why the customer should buy the product. What are its features? What can the products do? How long will the product last? What are other customers saying about the product? Does it come with a guarantee or a warranty? These are just some of the things that customers would like to know. And you need to provide them with clear and straightforward answers.

As you implement the strategies above, I would recommend that you track and keep a log of your progress. Building a website isn't always a one task job. A lot of the time it's all about refinement to create the best version. Of course that changes over time as well so you need to stay relevant. It's important that you identify the methods that are improving your conversion rates so that you can focus more of your attention on them.

Chapter 8:
How to Drive Consistent Sales through Email Marketing

Email marketing is among the oldest online marketing strategies. There's a reason why it has lasted so long and remains as relevant today as it was twenty years ago. It works. It increases sales. It improves conversion rates. It's as simple as that. If you want to maintain your customer base, email marketing is a great way to achieve it. In this chapter, we are going to look into some of the things you can do to generate more results from email marketing.

1. Utilize personalization to improve customer retention.

Email personalization involves creating messages that cater to the needs and wants of the recipients. If you have customers from various demographics, you should customize your messages to cater to each demographic. Make sure that your email copy reads like it was written for a human. A common mistake among new email marketers is that they make use of generic messages that they then send in bulk to all their customers no matter how segmented these customers are. This strategy is like shooting a shotgun into the dark hoping that a shrapnel will find its mark. It doesn't make any sense at all. So what you need to do is personalize your messages based on the sectors, segments, or types of recipients you are sending them to.

2. Take the time to craft catchy and interesting subject lines.

When you receive a message in your inbox, the first thing you read is the subject line, right? If the subject line doesn't interest you, you either mark the message as "read" even though you didn't actually read it or you send it straight to the trash file. You don't want this to happen to the messages that you send to your email list. The subject line is so important that some marketers spend more time writing and rewriting it than writing the message itself. Make people curious and interested to open your emails.

3. Add dynamic content to your messages.

Simply put, dynamic content is HTML plated within the message that changes and adapts based on the end user or recipient. Dynamic content plays a very important role in increasing user engagement. There are dozens of dynamic content tools that you can use to make the process easier. Such tools include Act-On, Avari, Bluecore, Boomtrain, Cordial, Kickdynamic, LiveIntent, and Movable Ink. Most of these tools charge for their services but the expense is trivial compared to the additional sales that you can generate because of them.

4. Track recipient behavior with analytics.

Install tracking snippets in your email campaigns so that you can see how your recipients are interacting with your messages. With tracking, you can learn which links are being clicked, which sections of the message are getting the most attention, and which segments of recipients have the highest engagement rates. With the data you gather through tracking, you can further improve your email campaigns in order to generate better results in the next campaigns.

5. Implement A/B testing in your email campaigns.

A/B testing refers to the marketing practice of using two different email ad copies with the intention of tracking them and learning which ad copy generates better results. For example, you can use images in the first copy and use no images in the second copy. You send the ad copies to the same numbers of recipients. You then measure how recipients interact with the ad copies. At the end of the campaign, you should be able to identify which copy generated better engagement and better results.

6. Invest in automated email

Many if not all of the above tasks can be automated and there are specific email programs to take care of that. When someone enters their email the automation takes care of everything. It will send them a chain of emails over time that you set up once. You can then track the results in the program and fine tune as you go. Check out Aweber, Mailchimp or Mailerlite.

As you may have realized by now, email marketing can be a time-consuming endeavour. You must be willing to invest a lot of your time and resources into your email campaigns. The time investment may be huge but the rewards can be huge as well if you do things properly. In fact, email marketing is so effective for a lot of online entrepreneurs that they generate most of their sales from their email campaigns. The point here is that email marketing can be a significant source of sales for your internet business.

Conclusion:
Now Is the Time to Take Action

If you've read this book in its entirety, then you are more than prepared to get your online business to the next level. With the strategies, tips, and advice I have provided in this book, you can build and grow a six-figure business.

That's not an exaggeration. You can definitely earn thousands of dollars every week from your business if you play your cards right. It's going to be a slow start but if you apply what we have discussed here, you can increase your numbers, improve your sales, ramp up your conversions, and earn serious money.

However, these things will only happen if you take action. All the strategies I have discussed in this book mean nothing if you don't apply them. As the saying goes, action speaks louder than words. Go over the chapters again if you have to. Just make sure to implement the strategies the way we have tackled them in this book.

Last but not the least, I would like to thank you for availing and reading this book. It means a lot to me. I hope that you found here the type of value that you were looking for. And I need one last favor from you. If you know of someone who might also be interested in reading this book, feel free to recommend this book to him or her. Thank you and good luck with your online business.

Thanks for Reading!

What did you think of, **Internet Marketing: Grow Your Business, Build a Brand, Make Money Online and Sell Almost Anything!**

I know you could have picked any number of books to read, but you picked this book and for that I am extremely grateful.

I hope that it added at value and quality to your everyday life. If so, it would be really nice if you could share this book with your friends and family by posting to Facebook and Twitter.

If you enjoyed this book and found some benefit in reading this, I'd like to hear from you and hope that you could take some time to post a review. Your feedback and support will help this author to greatly improve his writing craft for future projects and make this book even better.

I want you, the reader, to know that your review is very important and so, if you'd like to leave a review, all you have to do is click here and away you go. I wish you all the best in your future success!

Thank you and good luck!

William Swain

Claim your FREE Audiobook Now

The Ultimate Guide to Make Money Onlines

Grab your chance to own this comprehensive two audiobook bundle by Max Lane, covering everything you need to know about how to make money online and passive income ideas.

Including:

- *Make Money Online: Twelve Proven Methods to Earn Passive Income and Work from Anywhere in the World*
- *The Fastlane to Make Money Online: How to Write a Book and Make Passive Income with Self Publishing, Audiobooks and More*

Do you want to learn how to make money online consistently? Without a lot of fuss, scams, or investing any money?

If so - you've come to the right place....

THE ULTIMATE GUIDE TO MAKE MONEY ONLINE

Build a Passive Income Fortune with Kindle Publishing, Amazon FBA, Affiliate Marketing, Dropshipping, YouTube, Udemy, Blogging, Shopify and much more

How You Can Go From Zero To $1,000/Month In The Next 30 Days...

Find Out More